100 Classic Golf Tips

100 C
Golf

Edited by *Christopher Obetz* with *Matthew Rudy*

Drawings by
Anthony Ravielli

Foreword by
Tom Watson

lassic

Tips

Conte

nts

AFTER GRADUATING from Stanford, I immediately joined the professional golf tour. Throughout my years walking the fairways of the world, I have been privileged to experience incredible natural beauty united with landscape design and golf course architecture. I have watched golf's greats at their best and sometimes even their worst moments. Golf has afforded me the opportunity to make many friends I might never have had and witness genius both on and off the green.

One of the people who I was privileged to meet along the way was Anthony Ravielli. A small man with coke-bottle glasses and plaid shirts, Tony, as his friends called him, became a dear friend and my artistic curator. When it came time to put together the team for *Getting Up and Down: How to Save Strokes from Forty Yards and In*, after my 1982 U.S. Open win at Pebble Beach, there was no doubt who to go to for illustration: Anthony Ravielli.

Ironically, fifty years have passed since the legendary golf instruction book, *Five Lessons: The Modern Fundamentals of Golf*, was published. When Ben Hogan decided to analyze the swing, put it into words, and create the visual document, he sought out Tony. Hogan, being the ultimate perfectionist, wouldn't have had it any other way. Admiring Tony's work for both *Sports Illustrated* and *Golf Digest*, Hogan created the perfect recipe, including the words of Herbert Warren Wind and what would soon become the most recognized golf-instruction illustrations ever created.

Through his unparalleled knowledge of anatomy, Tony was able to capture the nuances of the swing, making it clear for the reader to follow along with the instructional tips and provide a perfect visual document to emulate. When it came time for Nick Seitz and myself to share the lessons I have learned every step of the way—from tee to green, rough to bunker—there was no doubt, Tony was our go to selection.

Over our fifteen years of working together, from the early 80s and into the mid-90s, I came to know the work of Tony and the man behind the glasses. A tireless artist and stickler for details, Tony delivered his

best in each illustration. When Christopher asked me to write the foreword for *100 Classic Golf Tips*, I was once again delighted to know that golf's vault of one-of-a-kind Raviellis would be opened for all to enjoy and learn from.

Reviving the historic illustrations of golf's legends, as seen on the scratchboards created over four decades, then pairing the illustrations with the eternal wisdom of golf's greatest professionals and instructors from *Golf Digest's* archives, was the ideal combination. Where technology may reduce distance or perhaps lessen the degree of an imperfect shot, there is no modern way to become a good golfer other than practice.

Developing a swing and understanding the nuances of each shot is essential. In *100 Classic Golf Tips*, the Ravielli illustrations walk the golfer through the "classic" fundamentals of each aspect of the swing and shots to follow. The instruction from golfing legends complements each illustration while maintaining simplicity, or what I like to refer to as the "basics." Together, they unlock the secrets of golf, and the success that comes from years of practice.

All of us who have known and worked with Tony sincerely appreciate his talent and the precision of his illustrations. Not only a premier artist, his passion and good will made anyone who worked with him a friend. We all miss you, Tony.

Wishing you all the best on and off the course, Tom Watson

100 TIPS

1.Grip

SHAFT IN PALM FOR PUTTING

How to develop consistency on the greens

In a putting stroke, the handle of the putter should be in your palms, along your lifelines. This lines up the shaft with your forearms—the proper position for the putter to swing on the right plane. I use a reverse-overlap grip on my putts: My left index finger extends outside my right hand and runs straight down the shaft, on top of the knuckles of my right hand. With the club in my lifelines and the reverse-overlap grip, I feel as if I have a lot of open space in some places between my hands and the grip. *Stan Utley*

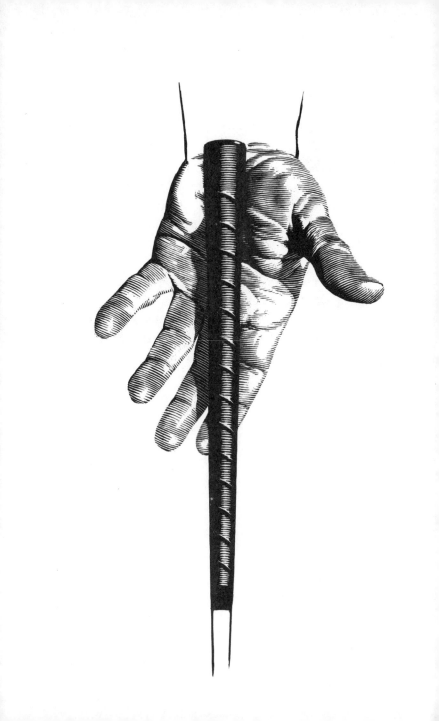

CHECKING YOUR GRIP

Strong, neutral or weak,
a good grip is unified

There are good players who have weak grips and good players who have strong grips. Tiger Woods has what I would call a "neutral" grip, which is between the two. All good grips obey one rule, though: Your palms must face each other as they hold the club. You shouldn't have a strong right hand and a weak left hand, or vice versa.

In a weak grip, the hands are turned so the back of the glove is almost hidden. With this grip, your hands should be a little higher at address. At the top of the swing, your left wrist should be flat so it makes a straight line with your left forearm.

In a strong grip, the back of the glove is almost entirely visible. With this grip, your hands should be a little lower at address, and at the top, your left wrist should be a little cupped, keeping the clubface parallel to the left arm at the top—a key to consistency.

Butch Harmon

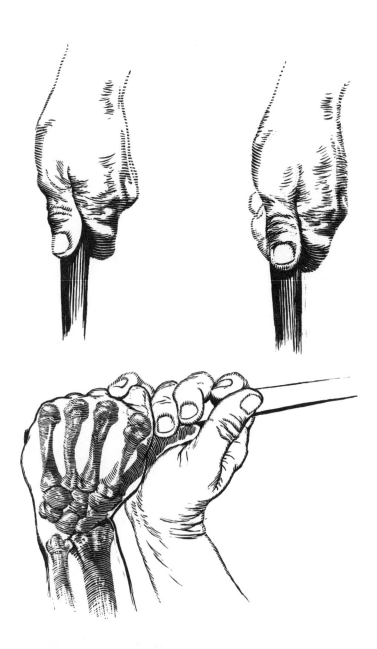

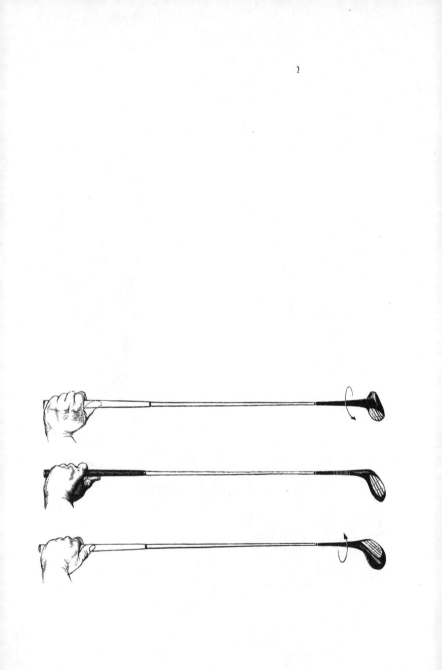

*How to check the position
of the clubface at the top of
the backswing*

I play best when I am what I believe to be "square":
left hand, wrist and forearm forming a straight line, and
thus setting the clubface midway between vertical and
horizontal. I can usually play fairly decently from an
"open" position, caused by a slight concave kink in my
left wrist angling the clubface closer to vertical than
horizontal. When a convex arching of my wrist at the
top "closes" the clubface so that it looks too far sky-
ward, I'm liable to be all over the park, and sometimes
beyond it. *Jack Nicklaus*

04

FINGER EXTENDED IN PUTTING

A simple move for improved control of the stroke

I certainly don't claim to have invented this grip, with the right forefinger extending own the shaft of the putter, but I do use it for greater control. It just gives me a little more feeling of command. I use an interlocking grip, the same as in my regular swing, but extend my finger. *Nancy Lopez*

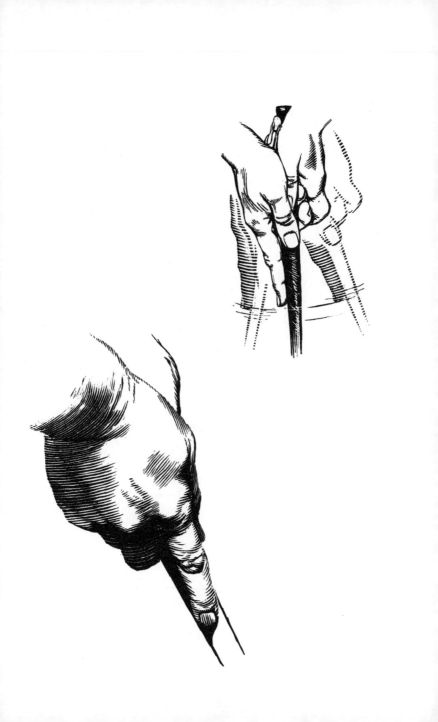

LINE UP THE PALMS

How to make sure your hands work together during the swing

Proper positioning of the hands is more important than most club golfers realize; it's more important even than they will make themselves accept. Make sure your hands are unified on the grip, with your palms more or less facing each other and your right palm facing roughly in the same direction as the clubface. ***Byron Nelson***

STRONG GRIP TO DRAW

A simple adjustment produces more power

Most women tend to cut the ball, and if this is the case, they must not be frightened of adopting a powerful grip. The left hand particularly should be placed well on top of the shaft, with as many as three knuckles showing and the thumb well to the right side of the grip. The shaft should be held firmly in both the palm and fingers, and there should be a feeling that the club is nestling deep in the hand so the fingers can really hold on to it. **John Jacobs**

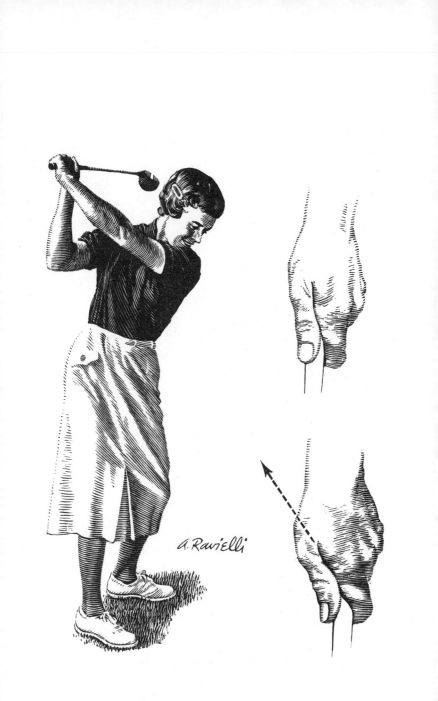

BASEBALL GRIP

Ten-finger hold promotes
a tension-free swing

I contend that most of the
tension built up in the average golfer stems directly from
the use of the Vardon, or overlapping, grip. I believe
most golfers would hit the ball straighter and farther if
they used the baseball grip. The left hand is placed on
the grip with the thumb slightly down the right side of
the shaft—the same as with a Vardon grip. All of the
fingers of the right hand are on the club, with the "V" of
the right hand pointing at the right shoulder. This makes
it easier for the average golfer to take the grip without
distorting any muscles. **Johnny Revolta**

A. Ravielli

08

LEFT-HAND GRIP IN FINGERS

How to take your grip the same correct way every time

Always establish your left-hand grip with the club positioned outside your left thigh, your left arm hanging naturally from your shoulder. See how my left hand is turned inward a bit? That's how nature intended it. All you do now is close your left hand on the club. As for the right hand, it simply joins the left as you move the club in front of your body in preparation for hitting the shot.

Beginning the grip process this way makes it easy to place the handle along the base of the fingers. It automatically establishes a neutral left-hand grip, with no rotation to the extreme right or left. Make this procedure a habit and you won't have to give your grip another thought. ***Butch Harmon***

09

LEFT THUMB TUCKS

*How to make sure your hands
fit together perfectly*

To get your hands working together, think of the left thumb fitting into the right palm, just as two pieces of wood are joined in tongue-and-groove fashion. First, take hold of the club with the left hand so the left thumb rests next to the top of the grip. Next, place your right hand on the underside of the grip, with the shaft crossing diagonally from the base of the little finger to the first joint of the index finger. Complete the grip by fitting the left thumb (tongue) into the hollow of the right palm, underneath the thumb pad (groove). ***David Leadbetter***

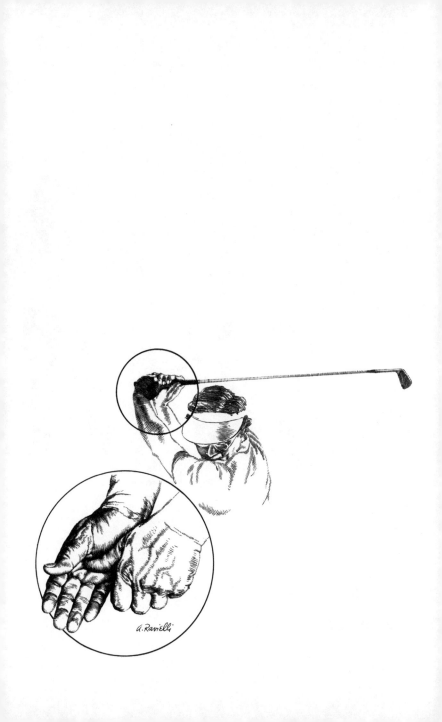

2.Setu

PROPER DISTANCE FROM THE BALL

How to set up correctly for every club in the bag

If you stand too close to the ball at address, your swing arc will be better suited to splitting logs than fairways. Stand too far away and you'll fight a continual—and losing—battle with balance.

First, stand erect but at ease, especially in the shoulders, with the club extended straight out in front of you at comfortable arm's length. Flex your knees slightly and stick your rear end out a little as you do so. Keep your head up, chin comfortably clear of your chest. Finally, without curving your back or dropping your hands, lean over from the hips. You are now the proper distance from the ball no matter which club you are holding. *Jack Nicklaus*

11

JACK'S BALL POSITION

How the Golden Bear makes address changes from club to club

With the driver, Jack Nicklaus likes his hands to be in line with the ball, his head well back. This encourages him to apply the clubhead to a teed-up ball with a slightly upward arc. His stance is a bit wider than his shoulders, so his feet are engaged. With a 5-iron, his hands are in the same position relative to his left leg. He likes to make shallow divots by tilting his upper body back slightly. For a wedge shot, his hands are still in the same position relative to his left thigh, but his stance is narrower. *Jim Flick*

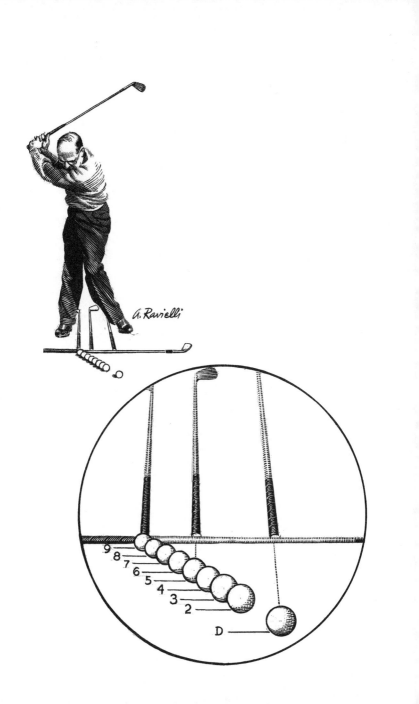

HIT DOWN
SLIGHTLY WITH
FAIRWAY WOODS

*A shorter shaft requires a steeper
swing vs. a driver swing*

The fairway woods should be used just like every other
club in the bag except the driver and putter—with a
descending angle of approach to the ball. In simple
terms, you hit down to make the ball go up. Too many
players do it in the opposite fashion—they try to swing
up with their fairway woods as if they were using a
driver with the ball on a tee. **Tom Kite**

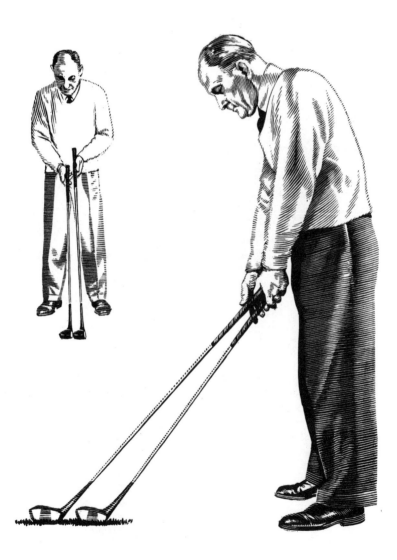

13

IMPORTANCE OF WIDTH

How to set up for a full turn and promote good balance

You will strengthen your swing greatly by adopting a stance width that enables you to turn fully in the back-swing without rolling to the outside of your right foot. The proper width also doesn't force you onto the outside edge of your left foot before the ball is struck. For most golfers, including me, that ideal occurs with the longest clubs when the feet are set apart about shoulder width at the centers of the heels. *Jack Nicklaus*

BALANCED SETUP

Keys to a powerful,
free-flowing swing

Jack Nicklaus is in absolutely super balance. His weight is distributed evenly between his two feet—perhaps slightly favoring his left. He stations his weight equally between the ball and the heel of each foot. He doesn't lean forward or back. This excellent weight distribution, along with a slight flex at the knees, allows the free footwork and leg action during the swing that are so necessary for building maximum clubhead speed. ***Byron Nelson***

15

PICK THE MODEL
THAT SUITS YOU

*For best results, alter address
position according to your build*

Many, many players try to emulate a player they like,
a Nicklaus or whomever, or pick out a swing style that
may be in vogue at the moment, but they may not have
the body type or physical or mental ability to swing
that way. Instead, every player's approach needs to
be tailored to his needs and stage of development.

Jim Flick

16

PLANE LANGUAGE

How the club's position at address determines the swing's proper plane

The plane on which you swing is established chiefly by your address position. As you stand to the ball comfortably and squarely, neither cramped nor reaching, your left arm and club more or less form a continuous straight line. The angle of that line relative to the vertical is the "ideal" plane at which to swing the club up and down with your arms.

John Jacobs

A. Ravielli

PRE-SHOT ROUTINE

*For improved focus
and to avoid mental errors,
shorter is better*

When it comes to picking the shot and club you're going to hit, don't overthink. Consider the lie, the target and any trouble in your way, but keep it simple. Once you make a decision, focus only on what you need to do — no second-guessing. If you feel nervous or think your swing is getting a little quick, take one more club and swing smoothly. *Annika Sorenstam*

CONTROLLING TRAJECTORY

Make small changes to hit shots higher or lower

Most players know how far they hit a certain club. But ask them to change a shot's height and you introduce some doubt. Changing your trajectory isn't complicated at all: Do it with your finish. When I want to hit a low 150-yard shot, I'll choose more club—a 7-iron for me— and move the ball back in my stance about an inch. I'll grip down on the handle slightly for more control, then keep my finish very low. That reduces the effective loft of the club and creates a lower shot.

For more height, I move the ball a little more forward and make a higher finish. The highest finish you see on the left is my three-quarter finish. I normally hit a 7-iron 165 yards. With this swing, I hit it about 155. I can use this for into-the-wind shots or if I'm between clubs. *Mike McGetrick*

SQUARE SETUP

*Line up the clubface first,
then the body*

The best way to help ensure
that your clubhead will be moving on line during impact is to set up to the ball correctly. It is important
that you realize that setup takes in aim and stance.
First you aim the clubface online behind the ball, and
then face yourself at a 90-degree angle to your clubface. With your clubface on target, any line across
your heels, knees, hips or shoulders should be
parallel to the line that runs through the ball to your
target. *John Jacobs*

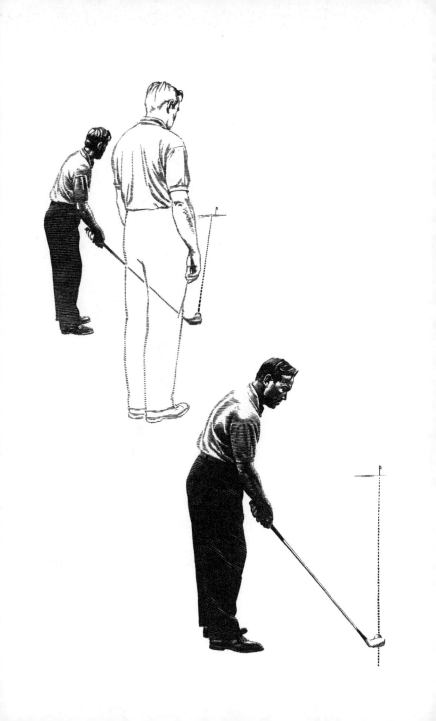

20

ALIGNMENT PROCEDURE

Line up all your body parts square to the target

Setting up involves a careful ritual: You grip the club correctly. Maintaining that correct grip, you aim the club correctly by placing it behind the ball so that its bottom edge is exactly at a right angle to your target. Then, you arrange your arms and limbs in the position that most easily and naturally allows you to swing along the line established by the aim of the clubface. This means simply that you stand with your shoulders, chest, hips, knees and feet square to the clubface.

John Jacobs

PUT SOME LIFE INTO YOUR FEET

Check the angle of your right foot to promote the proper leg action

You can't move your feet properly if they're uncomfortably angled in your stance; similarly, you can't roll them if there's no liveliness in them. Many pivot problems can be traced to leaden or dormant feet. Sometimes golfers try so hard to build a solid stance that they almost glue their feet firmly into the ground and thereby cut them out of the swing entirely. **Sam Snead**

A. Ravielli

CORRECT WEIGHT DISTRIBUTION

Set up with a lower right side to help pre-set a full coil

To hit the ball powerfully, you have to get behind the ball and stay behind it. A good setup helps you do that. In a bad setup position, my spine is tilted forward, my right shoulder is higher than my left, and my head is in front of the ball. Most of my weight is on my left side. From here, I'll have to sway to shift my weight—not good—or I'll have a reverse weight shift.

   In a good setup position, my spine tilts away from the target, my right shoulder is lower than my left, and my head is behind the ball. My weight is distributed fifty-fifty between my feet. From here, a simple turn shifts my weight properly and allows me to coil powerfully behind the ball. *Butch Harmon*

23

WIDER STANCE FOR POWER

How to set up and stay behind the ball for extra power

The secret to maxing out your power is in the setup. When I really want to rip it off the tee, I widen my stance by moving my right foot to the right an inch or two. This also moves my head farther behind the ball. I'll swing harder than usual—perhaps 90 percent compared with my normal 75 or 80—but I'm able to maintain my balance because of the wider stance.

It also helps to stay behind the ball through impact. The checkpoint for me is my right shoulder. If it's behind the ball through impact, then the rest of my upper body is, too. *Tiger Woods*

3.Swin

24

SWING LENGTH IS AUTOMATIC

Shorter club naturally leads to a shorter swing

The swings with the iron and wood are different, but we don't have to consciously do anything about it. To me, it's a little bit like a four-foot putt we are apt to strike and a forty-foot putt we would stroke. As an iron club gets shorter, we get a little more of a strike and less of a sweep, but it virtually all takes place automatically.

John Jacobs

25

COUNTING FOR RHYTHM

Make every swing, even with a driver, as smooth as a wedge

I seldom hit a shot very hard, and I seldom hit one very soft. This is particularly true with my wedges, mainly because I have shots to cover many distances. When you press too hard, you risk poor contact and wild shots. To set your tempo, try my one-two-three practice swing: Count one-two-three as you swing to the top, then one-two-three to the finish. It'll keep your speed in check. *Annika Sorenstam*

TAKEAWAY FAULTS

How to make a low, on-plane backswing

There are two faults you can make in the takeaway: You can pick the club up, or you can pull it back inside. When you pick the club up, your left shoulder drops. You tilt but don't really turn your shoulders. You hang on your left side, make a reverse pivot and either top the ball or chunk it.

When you take the club back inside, your left arm goes out away from your body, and halfway back it's above your right arm. The club goes behind your body and you have to loop it up and over on the downswing, causing slices or pulls. ***Butch Harmon***

SWING IN A BARREL

*How to prevent swaying
and reverse pivots*

For a strong coil and powerful
swing, the chest must move to the right, while the hips
stay relatively square. Think of it as moving the logo on
your shirt to the inside of your back knee. You'll be able
to do this only if you keep that knee flexed so it is ready
to receive the additional weight. Keep a consistent
spine tilt as well. If you lose that posture, your swing
path will be too steep and you'll drain all the power
from that coil. **Randy Smith**

SHOULDER TILT

Keep the left side low at the top of the backswing for accuracy

On full shots, my shoulder turn can be too level at the top of my backswing; a blocked shot to the right often results. You can really see this when I'm hitting my driver. Completing my backswing with the proper shoulder tilt—my left shoulder lower than my right—helps me swing the club down on plane and square the clubface at impact. *Se Ri Pak*

STAY DOWN WITH THE BODY

Maintain knee flex for solid contact and consistency

Staying down to the ball means keeping the body, rather than just the head, down through the hitting area. To do this, keep the knees flexed, the left side leading and the head back during impact and beyond. The right side will come down and under instead of up and around on the forward swing. *Byron Nelson*

30

HEAD IS THE SWING'S CENTER

How to deliver the clubhead to the ball properly every time

The head is the hub of the swing, the axis of the club's rotation around the body. Move the axis and you move the arc along with it. This may not make consistent clubhead delivery impossible, but it sure adds to the challenge. *Jack Nicklaus*

THE SWING'S ARC

*How to create extension
in the swing*

Tiger Woods often talks about getting "width" on the backswing. The proper extension of the left arm is a source of power because it helps create a wide arc to the swing. While this can be great advice, many players apply it incorrectly and extend themselves into trouble. The left arm goes wide, but the body center stays at home. This disconnect leads to poor arm location on the backswing, excessive tension in the left arm and limited body coil. People think they're doing something good when they have an overextended, rigid left arm, but what they're doing is losing all naturalness in the swing.

Keep a feeling of softness in the left arm as you swing the club back. This feeling will help you hinge your wrists. The left arm is the radius of your swing. Your shoulders, arm and hands should coil in sync. Be careful not to let that left arm overextend or work independently, which will change the setup radius of your swing. *Jim McLean*

EXCESSIVE
BODY ACTION

A tight, controlled turn in the
backswing promotes consistency

From address, keep your upper arms tight against your
upper torso. This way, your elbow stays tucked in,
making it physically impossible for you to overswing or
turn your hips and shoulders excessively. **Seve Ballesteros**

A. Ravielli

TURN, DON'T SLIDE

How to swing around the spine to develop the correct clubhead path

When a golfer sways his hips laterally away from the target going back, chances are fifty to one that he'll immediately spin around on his right hip and heel as he starts his forward swing. Unable to get his weight off his right foot, he's committed to an ugly "fire and fall back" routine, featuring a pronounced out-and-over movement of the right shoulder and an outside-in clubhead path through impact. The cure is simple and usually very effective. On your backswing, think of the lower spine as an axis, and turn your hips around that axis without letting any weight shift onto the outside of your right foot. **Jack Nicklaus**

34

RIGHT ELBOW MOVEMENT

How to unfold the right arm properly in the downswing

In most good golf swings, the right arm is slightly bent and the right elbow points down, not out, at impact. Otherwise, there's the danger that the right side will grab control of the swing, invariably with dire results. Past impact, however, the right arm does straighten and extend toward the target. To me, the movement feels very similar to that used in bowling or pitching a softball. It's a sweeping-through motion from which I get the feeling I could reach out and retrieve the flying ball with my right hand. **Jack Nicklaus**

G. Ravielli

35

WRIST POSITION AT THE TOP

Balanced position supports the club and sets up solid impact

In the ideal at-the-top position, both wrists are slightly cupped to support the club in balance. These matching angles are very similar to the V-shaped symmetry of a butterfly's wings. This solid position begins with a neutral grip at address, the creases between both thumbs and index fingers aligned parallel to one another and pointing toward the right shoulder. *David Leadbetter*

LEFT HEEL KEY

*Let flexibility determine its
movement in the backswing*

Tiger Woods is so flexible,
he's almost like the cartoon character Gumby. We've
sometimes had to work to keep him from turning too far
when he swings. Natalie Gulbis, a star on the LPGA
Tour, has the same "problem" with her swing: too much
flexibility. But most of us don't have that wonderful
problem. Especially as we get older, we lose flexibility
and our swing gets too short.

Here's a quick fix that will help you lengthen
your swing—without your having to raise a sweat down
at your local gym. Let your left heel come off the ground
if that helps you make a full backswing. The key word
here is "let." If you can make a full turn with your left
heel on the ground, do that. But don't let anyone tell
you that you can't play well if you pick up your heel
on the backswing. After all, the great Jack Nicklaus
picked up his heel quite a bit, as does Tom Watson.

Butch Harmon

37

MAKE A FULL TURN

Back should face the target to promote the correct swing shape

To be a consistent driver, you've got to hit the ball on the upswing. That's impossible if you don't make a full turn going back. Instead of hanging on your left side, get your shoulders turned and weight shifted—feel your weight move to your right heel. That puts you in position to hit up on the ball. ***Hank Haney***

FIRE OFF RIGHT FOOT ON DOWNSWING

How to utilize a major power source

Many players fail to utilize the power in their legs. Through impact, it's common to see the right foot remain planted, the right knee failing to drive toward the target. This lack of lower-body movement prevents the necessary weight transfer from taking place.

Imagine a balloon between your knees at address. As you swing back, keep the balloon firmly in place. You want to maintain resistance in your legs as you maximize coil. As the clubhead nears impact, pop the balloon by driving the right knee toward the left knee. **David Leadbetter**

39

DRIVE LEGS ON DOWNSWING

How to transfer weight and build power like a baseball home run hitter

To hit with power, you need to transfer your weight from your right side to your left side on the downswing. This is what teachers are talking about when they say, "Fire the right side." To do it, get your right elbow, hip and knee in line as you approach impact, and complete the weight transfer through the strike.

How do you know if you've fired your right side At impact your right heel is off the ground, your right knee is angled forward, pointing in front of the ball, and your right elbow has moved in front of your right hip. From this position, you can take advantage of the tremendous power you have stored in your legs and hips. *Jim McLean*

40

*How to build speed gradually
from the top for more power*

Speed is great in the golf swing except at the transition from backswing to downswing. Get too quick at the top and you'll tend to throw the clubhead away from your body and come over the top, which costs you power. One way to get a feel for a good transition is to think of the top of the backswing as a school zone. Keep your speed slow in the school zone, then push the accelerator as you come out of it, and floor it to highway speed. **Randy Smith**

41

STRAIGHT SPINE FOR CONSISTENCY

Maintain your spine angle throughout the swing

Because your spine is the axis of your swing (connecting your head with your hips), it must be relatively straight at address. Otherwise, it's like having an axle that's crooked—the wheels will wobble all over the place. **Chuck Cook**

42

RIGHT HAND AT TOP OF BACKSWING

Proper position keeps swing connected for consistency

When people talk about being connected at the top, they usually focus on the left arm—it's easy to see when the left arm is disconnected from the body. But don't forget about the right arm. You want to keep both arms up in front of your body. If you try too hard to connect your left arm to your chest, your right arm will disconnect and get too far behind you. Both arms should be connected the same amount. It should feel as if your right arm is bending straight upward. Imagine you're lifting a glass on a tray, your right arm forming a 90-degree angle at the elbow. From there, you need a little forearm rotation and shoulder turn and you'll be perfect—and connected—at the top. *Hank Haney*

A. Ravielli

KEEP THE HEAD STILL

*Excessive movement will cause
numerous faults*

A golfer can allow his head
to turn during the swing, provided he keeps it in one
position relative to the ball. However, in order to avoid
any lateral or up-and-down movement of the head, my
advice to the average golfer is that he try to keep his
head perfectly still. **Cary Middlecoff**

44

*How to initiate the proper
sequence in the downswing*

I like to think of the downswing
as a chain reaction. The first link in the chain is the
left side. It moves into and through the ball, pulling the
hands down, also into and through. The hands in turn
pull the clubhead down, into and through. The left side
must go through the shot. It shouldn't stop at the ball
and wait for the hands to catch up. The hands will do
that automatically. *Byron Nelson*

45

DON'T GET TOO WIDE GOING BACK

Set the wrists gradually in the takeaway

Both Tiger Woods and Davis Love III have tremendous width on their takeaways. That's one reason they hit the ball so far. But I've noticed that their swings go off when they get too wide going back. If you have this tendency, you should push your right hand as far as possible from your head at the top, with your right elbow bent about 90 degrees. That's easier to do if you have some gradual wrist cock earlier in the swing. There's still plenty of width there—and plenty of power to come. *Butch Harmon*

46

START DOWNSWING WITH LEFT KNEE

How to deliver the club property from inside the target line

If you're having trouble keeping your swing consistent when a match is on the line, key on your left knee to start your downswing. When you practice, remember to support your backswing with your right leg, then move your left knee and thigh first laterally, then rotationally, to your left. This allows your arms to drop the club inside the target line on the downswing for long and consistent shots. *Jim Flick*

INSIDE TO INSIDE
PATH

*How to keep the club on line
through impact*

Your club, hands and arms should stay well inside the
target line on the down—swing and follow-through.
With a proper shoulder turn, the clubhead will remain
inside the target line throughout the swing, but will pass
along that line in the hitting area. **Byron Nelson**

CHICKEN WING SLICE

Hit solid shots by keeping your left arm straight

A lot of people don't realize that when you slice the ball, what really happens is that the elbows spread. It's called the "chicken wing" finish because the left elbow is bent and jutting upward rather than straightened and turned under. That's a sure sign that the clubface has failed to close through impact. *David Leadbetter*

a. Ravielli

49

FOOT STABILITY THROUGH SWING

Miss the glass to stop spinning out and to push off the right foot correctly

The downswing starts from the ground up. Good footwork helps you stay down and behind the ball instead of moving ahead of it through impact. And it follows that the proper footwork leads to the proper leg action, and so on.

The key is your right foot and how it moves on the downswing. At the end of your backswing, the foot must be flat on the ground. From there, your weight should roll onto the inside of your right foot and, as your hips turn, you should push off of the instep and gradually turn the foot all the way up. At impact, your right heel should be slightly off the ground, and you should finish up on your right toe. **Hank Haney**

50

RELAXED TURN

*Swing with tension-free arms
for more clubhead speed*

The swinging of the arms
controls the shoulders. Unfortunately, many golfers
consciously turn the shoulders. That only creates
tension and interferes with the natural swinging of the
golf club. And we know that tension is a killer of
speed. Relaxed muscles are fast muscles. **Jim Flick**

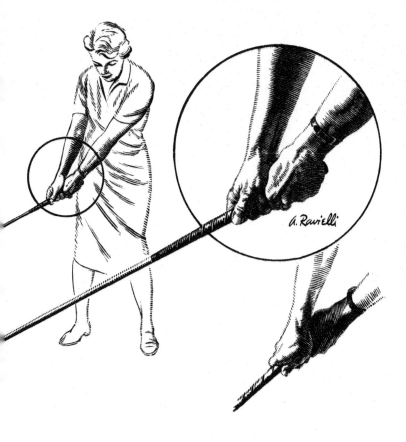

51

WOMEN: HIPS ARE KEY TO BIGGER TURN

How to develop more clubhead speed and produce more power

Many male golfers can make a big shoulder turn on the backswing with relatively little turning of the hips. That doesn't work for some women, perhaps, because they are naturally wider across the hips than the shoulders. For us to reach a position at the top with our backs facing the target, we have to really turn the hips as well. Restrict that hip action—and I'm afraid I see many club players doing so—and you're not going to be able to generate clubhead speed and power.

Kathy Whitworth

52

MORE POWERFUL IMPACT

Keep the left foot stable so you can rotate the clubface closed

The weak "flameout" off the tee is caused by an open clubface at impact and an angle of attack that's too steep. Somewhere in your golf swing the face of the clubhead rotates open and—unless you keep your left foot stable throughout the swing—is still open at impact.

To fix these problems, do three things:
1. Through impact, try to cover the ball with the toe of the club. 2. Add a bit of forearm rotation as you swing through impact—think of how you'd hit a forehand topspin smash playing tennis. 3. Don't cut down and across the ball and "come off the shot." Instead, swing from low to high. A shallower angle of attack is key to solid contact. With these changes, you'll soon be trading in that weak flameout for a powerful blast off the tee. *Jim McLean*

53

STAY CENTERED AS YOU TURN

How to make a more powerful coil

Simply put, if your head and hips move toward the target as your arms swing back, you're never going to hit good, strong golf shots. The reverse pivot prevents you from shifting your weight to the right side. On the full backswing, your left hip should move two or three inches away from its original position, and your upper center should move about six inches—enough so your sternum lines up over your right instep. **Jim McLean**

A. Ravielli

EXTENSION THROUGH IMPACT

Release the entire right side to generate power

To make the most of the power generated on the downswing, you must release your right side fully toward the target through impact, all the way to the finish. The feeling is very much like a boxer throwing a punch. When a boxer delivers a blow, he forcefully shifts his weight forward as he extends his right arm and shoulder toward the target.

Finish your golf swing with the same knockout punch. Fire through the ball by releasing your right side. Rotate your body all the way through the shot, so that your right shoulder is pointing toward the target at the completion of the follow-through.

David Leadbetter

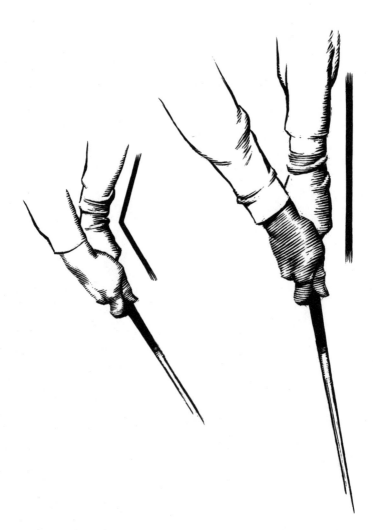

FLAT LEFT WRIST
THROUGH IMPACT

*How to generate more power
and encourage a straighter path*

Stop thinking about getting the clubhead to the ball
and start thinking about getting the handle past the
ball. For the average player, that means a fundamental
change in the position of the hands at impact. If you
flip the club, your trailing wrist flattens and the leading
wrist bends through impact. A good player's leading
wrist is flat and the trailing wrist is bent. ***Tom Ness***

56

TOUCH WRISTS FOR STRAIGHT SHOTS

How to release the club properly
through and past impact

Try to touch your left forearm with your right forearm as you strike the ball. They may not actually touch, but the thought will help you release the club. **Tom Watson**

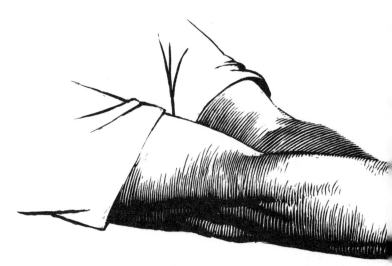

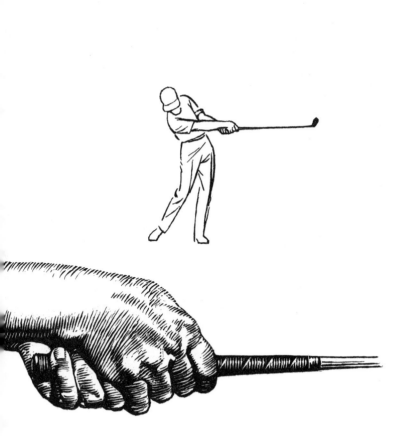

GOOD WRIST HINGE

How to use the hands correctly during the swing

The only type of wrist hinge needed while swinging the club is that which lifts and lowers the club. If the grip is proper, this hinging will occur at the base of the thumbs, producing wrinkles there, rather than at the base of the wrists. This wrist action gives the swing height and leverage, and lowers the clubhead to the ball during the downswing.

Eddie Merrins

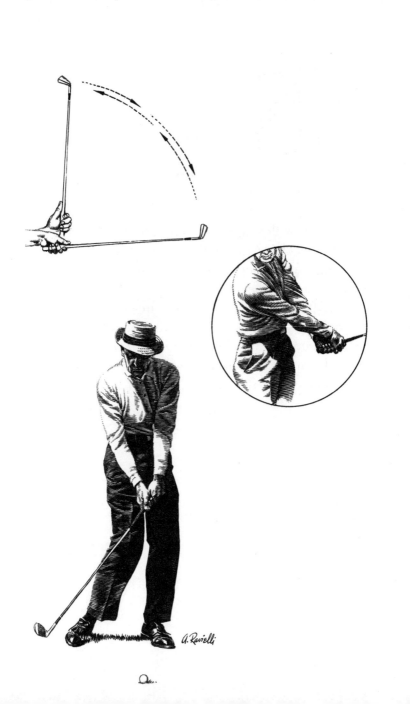

A. Ravielli

THE L SWING

How to store then release energy in the swing

The wrists act as hinges, forming angles between the arms and club in the move we call "L to L." Making half swings with your driver, create an L with your left forearm and the shaft when the club reaches parallel, then swing down, retaining that angle for as long as possible before whipping the club through impact.

After impact, re-form the L, this time between the right forearm and the clubshaft. This not only helps ensure you've transmitted maximum energy through impact, but also promotes the proper rotation of the forearms. ***David Leadbetter***

STAYING ON PLANE

How to swing the club in front of your body for consistency and control

Since I was a kid, I've had the same bad habit as a lot of other players struggling with swing plane. I'd get the club on plane at the top of my backswing, then drop it to the inside on the way down. That forced me to save the shot by flipping my hands over to square the clubface through impact. If my timing wasn't perfect—and it rarely was—I'd lose the shot either right or left.

Instead of dropping the club from the top of my backswing, now I focus on rotating my right forearm down and into my side. That helps me keep the club in front of my body and the clubshaft on the proper plane. Timing is taken out of the equation. I consistently hit the ball more accurately and control my distance more effectively. ***Tiger Woods***

4. Chip

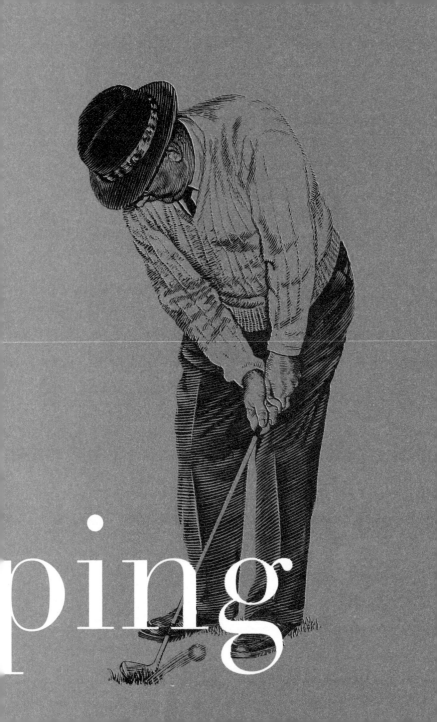

ping

60

DELICATE CHIP

Don't quit on the shot
for solid contact

Play this shot with a 9-iron or
pitching wedge, a grip of about the same firmness you'd
use to restrain a pet canary, and a chipping-type
stroke. Set your weight on your leading foot, the ball in
the center of your stance, and your hands ahead of the
clubface at address. Hold the clubface square throughout the short back- and throughswing. Because of the
softness of the shot, the tendency is to scoop at the ball
or quit on the stroke, so a good prime thought is to
swing down and through the ball. *Billy Casper*

61

LOFTED PITCH SETUP

*Open your stance, move
your ball position forward
to add height*

The address position is the key to executing this shot
properly. You have to give yourself the best possible
chance of creating the swing shape that will produce a
high trajectory. My weight is evenly balanced, maybe
just a touch more on the left side. My stance is open,
with my hands just ahead of the ball, which is opposite
of my left heel. Most amateurs find this shot difficult
because they place the ball back toward the right foot.

Jose Maria Olazabal

CHIPPING CONSISTENCY

How to use the method that provides the most control

Grip down on the clubs you select for short chip and pitch shots—almost to the steel —for greater control. Grip down to the exact same point on every club, to standardize the feel from one club to the next. Choke down consistently to make each club feel the same and to be able to predict the distance the ball travels with each club, with the same effort. The result is far steadier short game play. **Tom Watson**

ROTATE ON SHORT SHOTS

*Let your body move fluidly
to produce a natural stroke*

Many players try to bring the club back straight along
the target line, with an arms-only move. Instead, I let
the clubhead travel on its natural plane, on a curve
around my body. I rotate my forearms, fold my right
elbow and make a very small pivot. Having this lower-
body movement is more natural and fluid. My arms
aren't swinging the club back; I'm doing that with a
slight pivot of the knees and hips, and with forearm
rotation. The forearm rotation is going to feel extreme
when you first try it, but you'll be amazed at the
efficiency of your effort. **Stan Utley**

WRIST COCK
ON CHIPS

*Stiff arms and hands can
kill feel around the green*

Look at any of the great short game players, like Seve
Ballesteros or Phil Mickelson, and I guarantee you
you'll see wrist and hand action, and even a bit of leg
action—even on the smallest chips. The great short
game players all use soft hands and some arms. I'm not
talking about sloppy hand action, but it's definitely not
stiff-wristed or rigid. *Jim McLean*

65

STAND TALL FOR CRISP CONTACT

How to prevent fat and thin chips

Under-reach in your address position to avoid overreaching for the ball during the swing. Raise your suspension point by standing taller and extend your arms by gripping farther down the club. Hold the club lightly with the bottom of the clubhead about a quarter of an inch above the bottom of the ball. These adjustments let you swing freely without fear of catching the turf behind the ball. **Paul Runyan**

66

HOODING THE FACE
FROM ROUGH

*How to escape the long grass
with a setup change*

The main problem to overcome when playing out of
rough is the long grass, which, on a normal swing, will
catch between the clubface and the ball during impact.
Select a more lofted club and hood the face by playing
the ball well back in your stance. This will automatically give you a more upright backswing and permit
you to beat down and through the ball. It will give you
maximum contact with the ball through a minimum of
grass. **Doug Ford**

67

SWING LEFT SIDE THROUGH ROUGH

Keep the club moving through the grass for solid contact

This is not a difficult shot. You simply keep the left hand going toward the hole, accelerating it through the impact area and forcing the ball out. The left hand guides the club, almost as you would with a putt, and keeps the shot on line. **Dave Stockton**

CHIPPING FROM A BAD LIE

Favor the left side to promote crisp contact

The worse the lie, the farther to the right of the stance's center you should play the ball, the more your weight should favor your left side, the more your hands should be positioned left of the ball, and the higher-numbered the club you'll need to make the ball fly a given height.
Paul Runyan

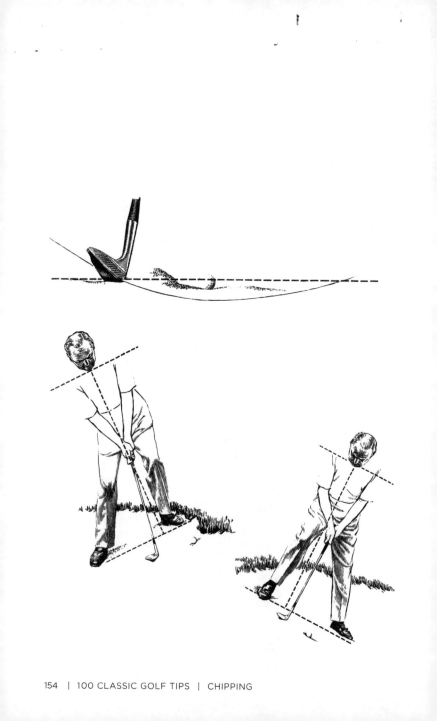

69

DOWNHILL EXPLOSION SHOT

How to align your body with the slope

The unfortunate tendency on downhill greenside bunker shots is to blade the ball, either by hitting it before the sand or by bouncing the club off the sand and into the ball (uphill bunker shots are easier). When playing the downhill shot, setup is critical. I align my body with the slope of the sand. My left shoulder is lower than my right shoulder. (If you drew lines through my shoulders and feet, the lines would be parallel.) My weight is on the inside of my left foot. I play the ball in the center of my stance, opening my body and the clubface slightly.

On the backswing I set my wrists a little more quickly and take the club up abruptly with my arms. Swinging down I make sure to hit behind the ball the same as I would on a level bunker shot. I follow through down the slope, keeping the clubface open and as low as possible. What I've done is change my address position and the arc of the clubhead to conform to the downslope. I expect the ball to come out lower than usual with more roll. *Tom Watson*

70

MAKE SMART CHOICES FROM HEAVY ROUGH

Laying up is often the high-percentage play

There are many times when a golfer should swallow his pride. Being faced with a bad lie in the rough is clearly such an occasion. If you can't see your ball from ten yards away, think about hacking it out into the fairway. Play the ball back in your stance. Aim for a spot in the fairway that gives you a good angle to the pin. Make a steeper swing than you might from a normal wedge shot from the fairway. **Mark O'Meara**

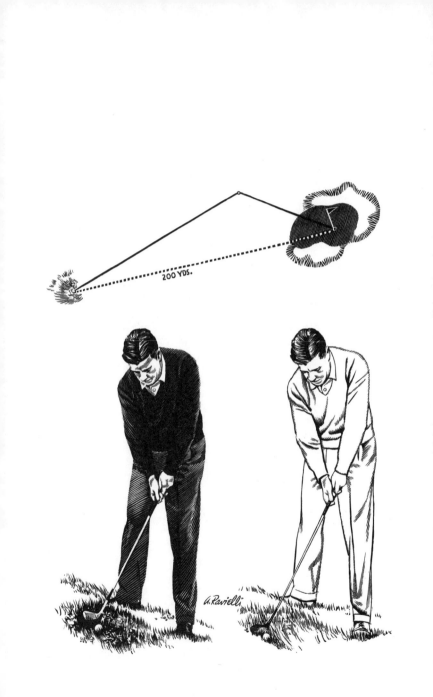

200 YDS.

71

THE TOWEL DRILL

How to use a target during practice to sharpen your short game

Payne Stewart always hated to work on the routine shots. So I gave him the Towel Drill to make the boring chips seem fun. Wet a towel (so it stays put) and lay it on the green about a third of the way to the hole. Try to chip the ball so it lands on the towel and rolls to the hole. This drill encourages you to keep the ball down and start it rolling as soon as possible. Try to get nine out of ten to hit the towel and stop near the hole.

Chuck Cook

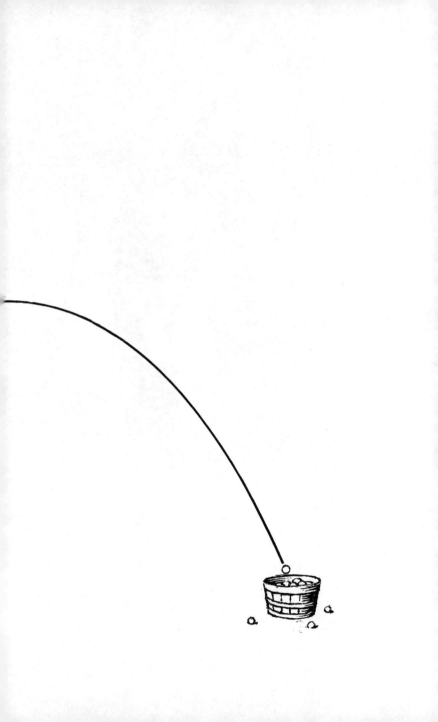

5.Putti

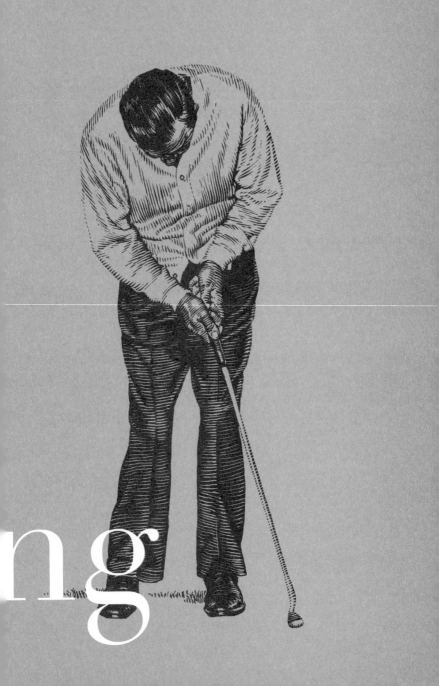

ng

72

*No matter how you look at it,
remember to factor in speed*

Speed as well as slope affects
the choice of path. If such factors as wet grass, long
grass, uphill terrain or a short distance to cover call for
a fairly aggressive speed, you should allow for less
sidehill curve. If a slick surface or a good deal of
length in the slope call for a more conservative atti-
tude—a slower rolling ball that dies at the cup—you
need to allow for more curve. ***Jim Flick***

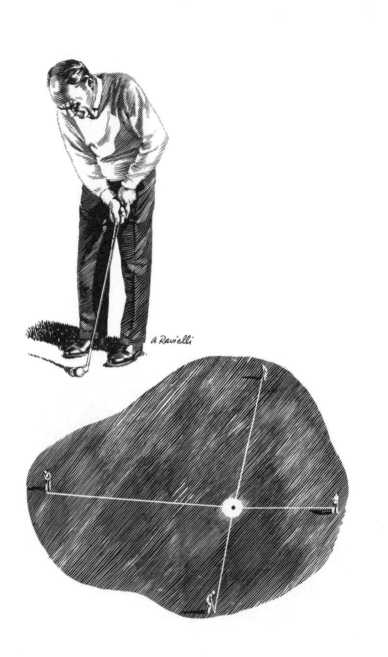

73

PRACTICE GREEN

*Surround the hole to make
more short putts*

One of my favorite drills is
building a putting clock of ten balls in a three-foot circle
around the hole. Each one of those ten putts has a
different, subtle break. Jackie Burke showed me this
setup, and he challenged me to make 100 putts in a row.
It took me a couple of weeks of trying, but I finally did it.
Now, I won't leave the practice green until I make those
100 in a row. *Phil Mickelson*

74

DIRECTION AND DISTANCE

The two keys for holing more putts

To hole putts, you have to get two things right—distance and direction. Trying to think about both at once can cause confusion or overemphasis on one element at the expense of the other. First, make up your mind once and for all about direction as you read the lie of the surrounding land, the grain of the grass and the slopes between the ball and the cup. As you begin to walk up to the ball, switch your mind away from direction and onto distance. *Jack Nicklaus*

DETERMINING SLOPE

How to make more putts over time

The art of judging slope and speed is not entirely God-given. It is possible to a great degree to develop the faculty. But the major part of any putting practice should be directed to that end rather than the development of a perfectly accurate stroke. If day-in and day-out a man will concentrate upon hitting the ball on the line he thinks is the right one, and with the speed he thinks is proper, and if he will let the luck and breaks take care of themselves, he will soon find that he is a much improved putter. ***Bobby Jones***

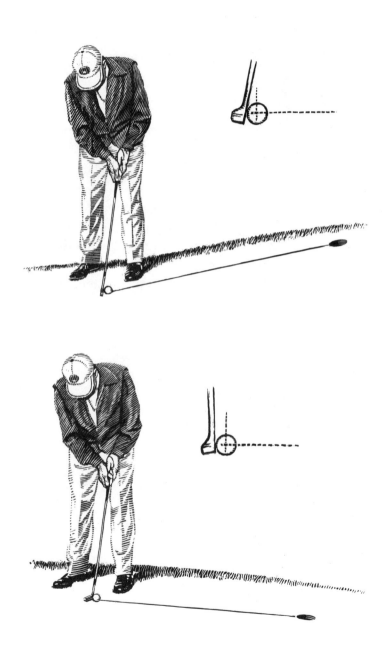

PUTTING
STROKE BASICS

*How to control the motion
with the left arm and hand*

We liken the putting stroke to the swinging of a pendulum. The stroke is done with the arms. It's a two-sided action, with the left hand and arm dominating while the right hand rests lightly on the club and stabilizes the stroke. You should feel you are using a one-lever system, stroking through the ball with the left wrist stabilized and the left hand and arm remaining in line.

Jim Flick and Bob Toski

77

GETTING BEHIND THE PUTT

Set up to allow for a freer stroke, like tossing a ball

Your weight should be slightly toward your right side, which gives you the feeling of staying behind the ball and stroking more toward the hole. Your knees should be slightly flexed, your weight solidly distributed between the balls and heels of your feet. Your arms should hang, your elbows resting close to your body, a position that allows less error during the stroke, because your elbows aren't waving around in the air. *Jim Flick and Bob Toski*

a. Ravielli

THE PUTTING STROKE

*How to make a repeating
pendulum motion*

I putt with my arms, keeping my wrists firm throughout the stroke. Only on the exceptionally long putts will there be any hinging of the wrists going back or coming through. I make no special manipulations to try to keep the putterhead low during the swing. If you do that, you must extend your arms during the backswing and forward swing. This ruins the pendulum effect, puts more variables in your stroke, and makes it more difficult for you to strike the ball solidly. *Tom Watson*

TOE CONTACT ON FAST PUTTS

Miss the sweet spot intentionally on fast greens

When I am faced with fast greens, I use this little trick to give me more margin for error. I simply address and strike the putt off the toe of the blade. This has the effect of deadening the contact between club and ball. There is no need for me to alter my stroke or decelerate into the putt. I can, in effect, stroke the ball a little harder than if I were making contact on the sweet spot of the putter. *Jerry Pate*

80

SHORT PUTTING

*Focus on the target,
not the outcome*

Most misses in the four-foot range are because of what is going on in your mind. You already know this. But what you may not know is how to calm your mind and organize your thinking to rid yourself of anxiety as much as possible. The worst thing you can think about is the result—what it's going to cost you if you miss, or what it's going to gain you if you make it. Take dead aim, and wash all those thoughts of results from your mind. **Harvey Penick**

81

LONG PUTTING

*Make a free, rhythmic stroke
to develop feel for distance*

As you get farther from the hole, distance becomes more important than direction. Consequently, mechanics take a back seat to feel. Longer putts require a freer range of motion on both the backswing and follow-through. As a result, your hands can be a little more flexible to impart a liberal amount of swing to your stroke. But that hand action isn't intentional or excessive. I simply let my wrists hinge naturally on the backswing. ***Hale Irwin***

a. Ravielli

FRINGE PUTTING

*From off the green, hit the ball
harder than you think*

With the putter you have to hit
the ball firmer from the fringe. But how much firmer?
That's the $64,000 question. Most weekend players I
see don't hit it hard enough. Err on the side of hitting
it harder than you think you should. Make your regular putting stroke, accelerating through the ball and
keeping your head still until after the ball is gone.

Tom Watson

A. Ravielli

BERMUDA GRAIN

*How to read putts more
accurately on grainy
Bermuda greens*

How do you know when you need to account for grain
on a putt? Rub the surface of the practice green. If the
blades stand up when you go in one direction and sit
down when you go the opposite way, you're dealing
with grain. You can also check around the edge of the
hole: The blades will be leaning toward the setting
sun. The more pronounced the grain, the more you'll
have to account for it on your read and in your stroke.

Rick Smith

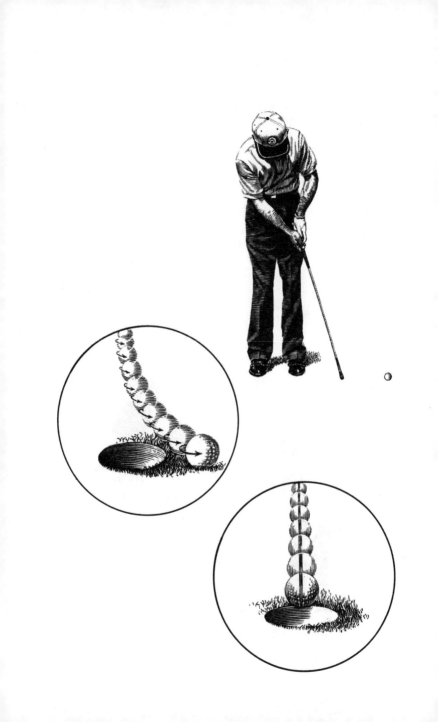

84

MARKING BALL OFF GREEN

How to read a putt from on the green and off

Golf architecture has evolved; greens now have more undulations and steeper slopes. As a result, today's putting strokes place a premium on smoothness and distance control, because much less effort is required to make the ball travel the equivalent distance, and there is a real possibility of hitting putts too far and even off the greens.

Almost without exception, every great putter I've ever seen has set up with his or her eyes directly above the ball or slightly inside it, toward the feet. That's the best way to see the putt's line. ***Stan Utley***

6.Sand

Shots

FRIED EGG LIE

Make a steep, descending blow to extricate the ball

Pick up the club and bring it down more sharply, striking directly the back of the ball with a clubface slightly more open than normal. Aiming at the crater edge is a good rule of thumb. Play for the ball to run, because you will get no backspin.

Sam Snead

86

BURIED LIE

*Adjust your setup
and allow for more roll*

Move the ball back in your stance to a point just inside your right heel. Grip the club a little more firmly than normal. Align the clubface square to the hole. Then turn your left shoulder under your chin. Combined with the adjusted ball position, this leads to your picking the club up quickly with your arms—not with an abrupt breaking of the wrists. Coming down, hit hard with your right hand. The club enters the sand at an acute angle and so your follow-through will be short. From soft sand, the ball will stop quicker. Harder sand causes the club to bounce, making more run inevitable. ***Seve Ballesteros***

HOW MUCH SAND TO TAKE

Make a shallower swing and carve out less sand

Most players have problems in the sand because of an incorrect approach—both mentally and physically. They try to hit an explosion shot, which causes them to swing down too steeply and dig out too much sand. As a result, they have to swing harder than is necessary and usually leave the ball in the sand or hit it way too far. On normal shots, I prefer to think of slicing the ball out of the sand with a slightly open clubface, much as you would peel an apple. If the clubface stays slightly open into the sand, the flange or bounce of the club comes into play and allows it to slide readily through the sand and under the ball. ***Byron Nelson***

THUMP THE SAND

*Open the face and swing
left for best results*

Many amateur players have the compulsion to move the ball and 300 pounds of sand onto the green. That's at least 299 too many. Line up with your feet slightly open to the target line and swing back along the line of your feet. Coming down again, focus on retaining the rotation of your left forearm through impact. That will hold the clubface open. Lightly thump the sand about two inches behind the ball as you swing the clubhead to the left. This shot is not a "splash" or an "explosion." **Nick Faldo**

A. Ravielli

SETTING YOUR FEET

89

*Dig into the sand to produce
a solid base for your swing*

You need good footing in the sand, especially if the sand is soft or sugary. The average player doesn't work his feet into the sand vigorously enough. Then playing the shot he slides around and loses his balance, making a bad shot very probable. You have to twist your feet into the sand until the movement of your feet is restricted. In soft sand, I'll twist my feet until the sand is well above the soles of my shoes. **Tom Watson**

90

OPEN STANCE

*Swing along your feet line
for soft, high bunker shots*

Set up to the ball in the sand
as you would for a normal wedge shot from the fairway.
Open your stance by turning your entire body to the
left until the clubface looks only slightly—a few degrees—to the right of the target. Maintaining a slightly
open clubface allows you to strike firmly with your
right hand without fear of closing the face and taking
too much sand. **Claude Harmon**

91

HANDS BACK

A consistent method from sand

I learned this unconventional bunker shot from Tom Pernice in the early 1980s, and it works great. I set up square to the target, with a very wide stance. My knees are bent—almost as if I am sitting in a low chair—which gets me down closer to the ball. I keep my upper spine tall, not hunched over. You know you're doing it right when your hands hang down near your knees. I'm slightly tilted toward the target, and I'll stay that way through the shot.

This setup helps me hit a consistent spot in the sand—about two inches behind the ball. I set up with my weight tilted left, hands behind the ball and the clubface square—different from a "standard" open clubface and forward hands. My method gives you more loft and more bounce on the back of your sand wedge, so the club skips through the sand and explodes the ball out. I hinge my wrists quickly and make a very narrow swing. I move the clubhead fast with my hands and wrists, instead of swinging my arms wide and hard. The wide stance and left tilt prevent a reverse weight shift— a recipe for disaster. *Stan Utley*

7.Othe

r Tips

HITTING THE WRONG BALL

How to handle the situation correctly before playing the next hole

Rule 15-3 is holy writ on this topic for stroke play. There is no penalty for playing a wrong ball in a hazard; there is a two-stroke penalty for playing it from outside the hazard, and then you must play the correct ball. If you hole out with a wrong ball, you may rectify the error if you have not played form the next tee (or, on the last hole, if you have not left the putting green).

Joe Dey

93

PLAYING VS. PRACTICING

*How to work on your game
more efficiently and effectively*

Practice is awfully important, especially to tournament
players. But there's a lot of wasted practice. I suggest
practicing as long as you are fresh. You'll do yourself
more harm than good if you hit balls after fatigue has
set in. Practice at first to correct mistakes. When the
mistakes are pretty much cured, practice should be
similar to playing. Hit a driver and then an iron, or a
drive, a fairway wood and an iron, just as though you
were playing a hole. *Harvey Penick*

A. Ravielli

94

DEVELOPING LEG STRENGTH

You don't need to hit balls to improve your swing

You need strong legs to support your upper body as you swing. Specifically, work on your quadriceps, the large muscles at the front of the thighs. You can use a fitness machine, or you can do an exercise I like that's easy to do at home, a few times a day.

All you need is a wall. You sit down, only not in a chair. Stand with your back against a wall, your feet about stance-width apart and a foot from the wall, your arms dangling at your sides.

Slowly lower yourself toward a sitting position by bending your knees. Don't go too far down at first—be sure you can make it back up. Hold the sitting position until you start to feel strain—a burning in your quads. As you get stronger, add repetitions and hold the position longer. Strong quads will keep you over the ball, with your head steady. **Tom Watson**

RELEASE THE HEAD THROUGH IMPACT

Balance and timing make the perfect swing

Good swings start in balance and finish in balance, so just learning to finish in a balance position will help your overall swing. One good characteristic is a slight reverse C—the back is arched a bit so the head is slightly farther from the target than the belt buckle. This position shows that the club came down on the right path in the forward swing.

Starting the forward swing should be a gradual acceleration. Build up the speed through impact instead of thinking in terms of fast starts or stops. When done correctly, you should be able to lift your right foot off the ground from your finish position.

Mike McGetrick

96

USING THE
BIG MUSCLES

*How to produce power
in the swing*

Whether an athlete is swinging a club, racquet, bat or
paddle, the best players control the hands and arms
with the big muscles of the body—the large muscles of
the legs, torso and shoulders—rather than with the
smaller muscles of the arms and hands. Proper use of
the body initially produces power, which is then transmitted through the arms and hands. *Jimmy Ballard*

A. Ravielli

MAKE THE FAIRWAY A BIGGER TARGET

Aim down one side and work the ball toward the middle

If you were to stand in the middle of a tee box and aim down the center of a fairway that's forty yards wide, you only allow yourself twenty yards of curvature. Anything more and you'll find rough or trees. But if you set up on the right side of the teeing ground and aim for the left edge of the fairway, you now can fade the ball up to forty yards and still find the fairway. You've doubled your margin for error. **Tom Weiskopf**

FADE SETUP

*How to hit it left to right
for more control*

If you turn your hands counter-clockwise or to the left on your grip, you will tend to pick the club up more sharply, taking it more straight back or perhaps outside the line, and a more upright swing will result. In the downswing, you will come at the ball more directly down the target line, your hands will not release as much or as quickly and you will tend to fade the ball. Use your same stance and setup posture with these variations. The only other adjustment you make is in your aim. **Mike Souchak**

99

SHANKS CURE

All you need is a simple prop to groove a fault-free swing

Place a headcover just outside the ball and hit some eight-irons, moving gradually from inside the target line on the downswing to along the target line at impact to back inside on the follow-through. If you hit the headcover before you hit the ball, you're still approaching impact from the outside—that's shank city. **Rick Smith**

100

*Visualize the shot,
feel it, then execute*

Imagination in golf originates from your eyes. You see the ball and the place where you want the shot to finish. Next, you make a mental note of the many variables that go into shot planning. Then you imagine the best route your ball should take to finish on target, and the flight pattern it should assume. Finally, you should imagine or sense how your swing should feel to produce this type of shot.

Horton Smith

A. Ravielli

First published in the
United States of America in 2007 by
Universe Publishing
A Division of
Rizzoli International Publications, Inc.
300 Park Avenue South
New York, NY 10010
www.rizzoliusa.com

2007 2008 2009 2010 / 10 9 8 7 6 5 4 3 2

Design by Opto

ISBN-13: 978-0-7893-1546-5

Library of Congress Control Number:
2006911244